The Power of Belief

Ridgely Goldsborough

The Power of Belief
by Ridgely Goldsborough

Revised Edition. Second Printing.
ISBN 0-9745696-0-7

For additional copies, visit:
www.AViewFromTheRidge.com

Cover Design: Tammy Sadler
Photo Credit: Donald Puckett

Printed in Canada.

3

Dedication & Acknowledgments

To my family, Ali, Linus and Camille, who constantly share their love and support throughout a process that all too often reminds me of a root canal. I can't imagine doing this without them.

Special thanks also to Aaron for his visionary leadership, guidance and friendship.

Contents

PROLOGUE

"You won't escape," said the mighty spider to the fly. "Tonight, I'll move my web. Tomorrow I will trap you."

"No, you won't," replied the fly. "I'm leaving very soon and you will never see me again. I'll travel a thousand miles to see the world."

"You're a tiny fly," smirked the spider. "You won't make ten miles, never mind a thousand."

"That's what you believe," smiled the fly. "Those that believe the same get caught in your sticky trap that leads nowhere. Not me. I believe otherwise and shall have a different fate."

The fly flew to a gatepost and waited. In due time a gentleman horseman came along at a trot. The tiny fly hopped on the horse's tail. They rode and rode and rode.

SECTION I

Why do we do what we do?
The Roots...

This wonderful creature called human being, like all creatures, has a basic make-up.

It has an organic component that moves it and drives it called the heart.

It has a logical component that logs and processes information called the brain.

These two components come together as the creature takes action. Each action creates an experience that takes data from the logical left side of the brain and processes it through the emotional right side in the form of a feeling. The sum of all feelings makes up the programming that runs the human being.

It's called a belief system.

Nothing happens without belief.

How does this programming work?

Where does it come from?

Who writes the code?

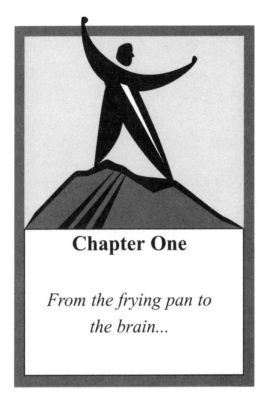

Chapter One

From the frying pan to the brain...

Man is made by his belief.
As he believes, so he is.

Bhagavad Gita

A tiny baby latches on to her mother's breast. Feelings of hunger, loneliness and fear transform into feelings of comfort, love and safety. Over time, the baby begins to understand that the breast produces milk, that it hides beneath several layers of clothing and that drinking from the breast relieves hunger pangs.

This knowledge however, does nothing to engender a feeling of comfort. It is simply knowledge. The feeling of comfort comes from the actual experience of drinking the milk wrapped in a mother's arms. Only by going through the act of drinking does the baby associate the mother's breast with comfort.

That *feeling*, forms the basis for an early belief, a belief that carries the fundamental message, *"mother's breast equals comfort."* The sheer knowledge of where the milk comes from has no influence on that belief.

Our beliefs stem from our feelings, not the information, education or data that we cram into our minds. Only when we take data and experiment with it through our actions, do we gain the necessary experience for that data to transform into a feeling, which in turn influences our belief system.

17

I hear and I forget. I see and I believe.
I do and I understand.

Confucius

All the books in the world will have no impact on your belief system unless you take action based on what you learn, go through an experience and feel the emotional side of that experience.

Understanding this concept carries profound implications. It suggests that *"book learning"* without life experience carries scarce weight other than as an intellectual exercise. It demonstrates the merit of *"street smarts"*—smarts based on experience, of *"wisdom of the ages"*—wisdom based on experience, of *"Grandpa's prophetic knee"*—prophecy based on experience. It validates why stories pack so much power as a teaching method, because a great story teller will take his listener on an emotional roller coaster, living the story through a series of experiences.

Each experience creates certain feelings, good, bad, positive, negative and everything in between. The sum total of these feelings molds and shapes our belief system, which dictates the way we behave going forward. Our belief system becomes a ***REPOSITORY OF ACCUMULATED FEELINGS.***

I do not believe that we can put into anyone ideas which are not in him (her) already.

Albert Schweizer

Consider a simple example. You purchase a new iron skillet for your kitchen. According to the advertisement, this skillet *"locks in the flavors of your favorite foods in no time flat."* Intellectually, you know that in order for *"flash cooking"* to take place, the skillet must get extremely hot. Still, you don't truly **believe it** until your hands physically touch the skillet handle and *feel* the heat.

How often have you looked at a pan on the stove, seen the flames beneath it and still felt the urge to lightly tap it with your finger to *"find out if it is truly hot?"*

That *feeling* of heat causes you to hold back from grabbing the body of the skillet and burning yourself. The mental knowledge that fire applied to iron generates enough heat to burn skin has no power in a vacuum. It only gains power based on the experience of touching the iron, that spawns the feeling of burning on the skin, that leads to a belief that says:

"Wow, if I do that again, I might feel the same painful sensation. Hmmm, hot pan burns. I should avoid grabbing it without mitts."

From the time of our creation, experience by experience, feeling by feeling, we build a belief system—a system so powerful that it reigns over us like a supreme monarch who dictates the way we think, talk and act from moment to moment, for the rest of our lives.

Chapter Two

*Parents, circumstances
and choices...*

Our convictions on important matters are not the result of knowledge or critical thought, nor, it may be added, are they often dictated by supposed self-interest. Most of them are pure prejudices in the proper sense of that word. We do not form them ourselves. They are the whisperings of "the voice of the herd."

James Harvey Robinson

Parents come with certain baggage. They carry the weight of ethnic origin along with trunk loads of personal prejudices, judgments and opinions based on their own life experience. Whether you hold a belief that you chose your parents, that they were pre-ordained or randomly plucked from the universe makes no difference. You have them, even if you don't know them or maintain little contact. Their belief system has an enormous influence on the early shaping of yours, either by commission because one or both of them took an active role in your development or by omission because, for whatever reason, they did not.

Let's start with ethnic origin. Each group and culture has certain generally accepted belief principles that influence their daily behavior. If your parents came from different backgrounds, you are affected by all of them. Even if your parents rebel against the "*traditions*" of their culture, still, that seldom insulates you from your other relatives who respect and follow those traditions. Your parents' childhood friends have children that become your peers. And so on. Where you come from makes a difference.

25

Fact of the matter is, there is no hip world; there is no straight world. There's a world, you see, which has people in it that believe in a variety of different things. Everybody believes in something and everybody, by virtue of the fact that they believe in something, use that something to support their own existence.

Frank Zappa

In addition, you will pick up your parents' philosophies and views on how the world turns and what role you play in the drama. If raised by someone other than your parents, you will adopt many of their views. As you grow older and develop your own perspectives you will likely rebel in an effort to assert your independence.

Here's the catch-22 faced by all of us: Despite our best intentions or deepest desires, without new programming **WE BECOME THE VERY THING WE RUN FROM**.

How many times have you done something that strikes you as peculiar only to stop with the sudden realization:

"Wow. I can't believe I just did that—that's such a 'Dad-ism' or 'Mom-ism'."

Without new programming, the product produced by any machine—human or otherwise—will never change. We become trapped in previously established programming, that of those who taught us. Patterns and behaviors repeat themselves in an endless, invariable cycle.

Added to our parents' influence, our childhood circumstances plant multiple seeds and notions in our minds, many of which germinate much later.

Seeing is believing all the world over.

Miguel De Cervantes

Common ways of thinking get logged onto our mental hard drive from the daily interactions in our environment. Without judging their value, simply note that they exist and that you have them. We will soon figure out whether they serve us or not and what we can do about them if they don't.

For example, affluent neighborhoods trigger certain thought patterns. Less affluent neighborhoods trigger others. A person that grows up in the city will likely learn more about social interplay than a person that grows up in the country, who may develop a deeper appreciation of the plant and animal world. Perhaps you grew up in a foreign country with an alien political government or live in a remote area with a staunch political bent. Your circumstances will naturally sire systems of thought.

Each time you take action based on any of the mentioned factors, your experience will translate into a feeling that impacts your belief system. Who and where we come from matters, at least from the standpoint of molding our beliefs. As we move into the process of re-shaping our belief system, understanding its origins helps us identify core beliefs more quickly and effectively.

Nothing is so firmly believed as what is least known.

Montaigne

Last, we get to the matter of choices. Throughout our youth, we face many choices, all of which are influenced by our circumstances and upbringing. Because we are human, we have been gifted with the unique blessing of free will. Therefore, despite the pull of our programming, when faced with a fork in the road, we often choose the path that flies in the face of what we have been taught.

We become our own teachers. We learn from those experiences, especially since our mistakes tend to produce stronger feelings than our good decisions that we take for granted. Each feeling gets logged onto our "*belief*" hard drive.

Here's the problem. Most of us perceive these daily choices as independent of each other. We fail to see the interconnectedness and believe that because of our free will, we could easily pick the other route when faced again with the same fork in the road.

Nothing could be farther from the truth. Each small choice breeds familiarity and a predisposition to repetition, to making the same choice again and again, or worse, to choosing the next step along a negative progression.

We are born believing. A man bears belief,
as a tree bears beauty.

Ralph Waldo Emerson

Consider this example. Coaxed by his buddies, at age nine young Johnny decides to smoke a cigarette. He suffers from coughing and gagging yet is rewarded (or so he deems in that moment) with the approval of his peers, *"the cool guys."* Before long, Johnny rationalizes the swiping of a few cigarettes from his mother's purse and soon thereafter, he snatches a five-dollar bill to buy his own pack. Two years later, Johnny graduates to marijuana in order to remain in the *"in crowd."* A few years after that, he exchanges marijuana for martinis, eventually settles on his own drink *"of choice,"* and becomes an alcoholic.

Too far fetched? I don't think so. Many people you know have likely followed this or a similar path to some type of addiction—a sobering thought (excuse the pun.)

In a void, each small decision carries little weight. Over time, the accumulation of choices leads to patterns almost impossible to break. Those that start in early childhood come into play more and more as time passes, building upon each other like snowflakes on a mountain side. A single flake matters very little in isolation. The accumulation of flakes leads to an avalanche.

> *Oh, what a tangled web we weave when first we practice to believe.*

Laurence J. Peter

We cannot slip back in time to change our parents, circumstances or choices. Their influence has placed a strangle hold on our belief system, one which only persistent, dogged determination will loosen and eventually remove.

Chapter Three

*The strands that
hold us together...*

The world we see that seems so insane is the result of a belief system that is not working. To perceive the world differently, we must be willing to change our belief system, let the past slip away, expand our sense of now and dissolve the fear in our minds.

Gerald G. Jampolsky

Picture each individual belief like a wire cable made up of tiny wire strands. Each time you repeat a behavior that triggers the same familiar feeling, you add a strand to the cable. Over time, that cable becomes virtually unbreakable under almost any circumstance. The longer you repeat the behavior, the more strands you add.

You cannot cut them off. They withstand the most devastating of all storms. Only a life and death tragedy such as a fatal illness or the loss of a loved one can threaten the strength of that cable.

By the time you become an adult, your life experiences will have twisted together enough strands to hold you up, in some shape or another. By the time you reach middle age, the number of strands could hold up the Brooklyn Bridge. The programming has enough data to sustain itself forever.

Continuously, life swirls on around you. The mind churns 24/7, logging experience after experience, filling more and more memory with feelings. We receive information at astronomical rates, faster and faster.

The fact that an opinion has been widely held is no evidence that it is not utterly absurd; indeed, in view of the silliness of the majority of mankind, a widespread belief is more often likely to be foolish than sensible.

Bertrand Russell

Once in while, we receive different data that causes us to experiment with a new type of action that leads to a new experience and makes a slight modification to our belief system.

What about the rest of the data? Where does it go? It doesn't simply disappear.

Of course not. It gets logged as well, strengthening the existing programming, adding more strands, building enough evidence to justify the same behavior and create the same output. The computer puts out exactly what it is supposed to according to the programming it receives. Flawless.

Unless of course, you don't like the output.

Consider the media barrage as an example. We live under constant reminder that we should stay healthy and fit. The *"body beautiful"* syndrome assaults us like a plague at every turn. We should *"eat right, exercise and get plenty of rest."* All of that makes sense, sounds *"believable."*

On the other hand, our pursuit of perfection tells us that we should do and be more, jet from one activity to another, always on the go. We have to

People everywhere enjoy believing things that they know are not true. It spares them the ordeal of thinking for themselves and taking responsibility for what they know.

Brooks Atkinson

give 110% to everything—family, career, health, spirituality, personal interests.

The stress brought on by *"keeping up with the Jones'"* expresses itself in direct rebellion to both fitness and this societal busy-ness.

Result? We overeat to comfort ourselves, suffer from unprecedented levels of obesity, become sedentary and further contribute to the very heart disease we seek to avoid. We run until we collapse, flop down onto the couch with a tub of Haagen-Dazs to watch television and recover from the chaos. Our actual experience leads to a different belief—the belief that we need rest and down time, because we feel tired, even deserving.

What do we see when we flip on the TV? More beautiful bodies with subtle admonitions of what we will miss out on if we don't have one, coupled with more reminders of the need to be perfect people who *"do it all"*—or face the consequence of feeling like a complete failure.

We can't win. We can't do it all. We can't live up to a fantasy picture. It's not real.

I never cease being dumbfounded by the unbelievable things people believe.

Leo Rosteu

THIS RELENTLESS PROGRAMMING HAS SET US UP TO FAIL.

We have been force-fed tremendous knowledge but given almost no wisdom. Few of us have any sense of balance and even fewer go after our dreams, choosing instead to live through fantastical lives of others, wanting, wishing, but never getting what we wish for.

How could we? Until we take control of the programming, we will never gain control over the output. We will bob along the sea of other peoples' beliefs like a cork on the Pacific Ocean. Though we many not sink, we will tumble with every wave, find ourselves frequently under water and spend most of our time aimlessly floating.

In order to regain control of our lives, we must be the ones writing the code. We have to get to a place where the programming serves us, gives us the output we want, leads us to our goals and dreams.

The only way to do that is to reform our beliefs.

SECTION II

What if you could have it all? The Reformation...

Imagine a thousand data operators in your mind, sitting at their stations and logging every bit of data that flows your way, every thought you think, every word you say, every action you take— the very thoughts, words and deeds that create the feelings that mold your belief system.

Imagine a thousand gnomes tugging at your heartstrings, pulling you in multiple directions, conflicted and confused.

You have no authority over the data processors.

You have no control over the gnomes.

The only thing you can regulate is the data itself.

What are you letting in?

Chapter Four

Stop the negative spiral...

A belief is like a guillotine,
just as heavy, just as light.

Frank Kafka

Beliefs bombard us from day one. In early childhood we have virtually no say in what they are or where they come from. Our parents and circumstances decide for us. We do our best to endure the assault.

Throughout our youth the speed and amount of information we receive increases much faster than our ability to sort and manage it all. We absorb it like sponges until we saturate, pregnant with the expectations and mandates of others.

Although adulthood signals the official cutting of parental and scholastic ties, by that time our programming has sunk deep and defining roots, roots made up of thousands of experiences, each like a piece of mental computer code that requires another piece of code to neutralize it and a third piece to make any lasting change in the programming. To make matters worse, many powerful behavior patterns take hold and strengthen each time you act in accordance with those patterns. We build tendencies and habits. To crack that code and alter the overall programming, we have to do three things:

We believe what we want to believe, what we like to believe, what suits our prejudices and fuels our passions.

Unknown

1) Stop reinforcing old code.

2) Begin inputting new code.

3) Build different patterns based on the new code—patterns that perpetuate its strengthening.

Imagine a person (it could be you) who grows up in a circle of influence that casts blame on others, complains and points the finger at people and circumstances outside themselves for all of their shortcomings and difficulties. You get conditioned for many years to follow those patterns.

One day, you read a book on personal responsibility, have a revelation that this finger-pointing tendency yields little fruit. You have a classic *"day of disgust,"* the painful realization that your life falls far short of what you want. You decide to stop casting blame and do something different, take charge of your life. The logical left side of the brain supports this decision—*"Hey, if a behavior yields poor results, stop doing it,"*—an intelligent, straightforward thought.

I know that most men, including those at ease with problems of the greatest complexity, can seldom accept even the most simplest and obvious truth, if it be such that it would oblige them to admit the falsity of conclusions which they have delighted in explaining to colleagues, which they have proudly taught to others, and which they have woven, thread by thread, into the fabric of their lives.

Leo Tolstoy

You feel great about this empowering decision, puff up inside with a renewed determination. That feeling impacts your belief system and leads to a strong line of code that reads *"I am powerful when I take personal responsibility. It feels great and allows me to believe in myself,"* or some variation on this theme. With fresh resolve, you forge into the world.

On the following day, senior management discovers a series of mistakes in your monthly reports, mistakes that cost your company a significant amount of money. Do you take responsibility, own up to the mistakes, knowing that to do so will cause you pain and suffering, or do you pass the buck as you have in the past?

The empowerment side of personal responsibility carries the realization of the painful consequences that go along with it. Will a single instance of personal responsibility alter a lifetime of blaming others? Probably not.

What if the stakes creep up, lead to potential termination on the job?

*There lies more faith in honest doubt
Believe me, than in half the creeds.*

Lord Alfred Tennyson

The problem compounds. In discussing the matter with family, what do you think they will recommend? Will your determination withstand the familiar assault?

Not a chance. It will fade into a forgotten corner.

Why? Because years of negative programming will grind out one isolated moment of enlightenment as fast as dark clouds obscure the brightest sun.

The reformation of our belief system, the re-writing of the code that governs us, won't happen overnight. It will take time, effort and exceptional commitment. Exceptional commitment will yield exceptional results. I invite you to become the exception.

The process has two fundamental steps. First, we have to *STOP THE NEGATIVE SPIRAL*. As my friend John Costino once said:

"You can't run uphill in a mudslide."

Before we can write new programming, we **MUST** stop adding to the old programming that gave us the poor results we seek to change. Our

Generally, the theories we believe we call facts, and the facts we disbelieve we call theories.

Felix Cohen

quest to re-craft ourselves involves a long and arduous climb. We don't need unwanted mud flowing down as we rise.

Once our feet stand on firm ground, we plan our upward ascent.

Understand that we will never completely quarantine the deluge of negativity. The key lies in having the mindset to minimize it, ferret it out with every opportunity, consciously cast it aside and keep casting it aside with relentless zeal.

Then we can re-build.

Chapter Five

Are you minding the gate?

Sometimes, believing that we're moving forward, we run blindly, like the hamster inside a wire wheel believes he's moving forward.

Unknown

Both positive and negative data streams our way in myriad waves. Some we govern, some we don't. We have little say in the content of the billboards that line our highways. We hear our favorite deejays comment on the crisis of the day. Friends remark on the economy and attempt to engage us in debate. Modern community dictates that we maintain a marginally informed state. No one lives in a bubble. All of this information challenges or reinforces our belief system.

Besides the daily barrage, who decides the rest?

We do. We determine what books to crack. We set the dial on the radio. We push the buttons on the remote. We choose who we spend time with. We decide where we live.

WE HAVE TOTAL POWER OVER WHAT WE READ, LISTEN TO AND WATCH, OVER WHO EARNS OUR TIME, OVER WHERE WE CHOOSE TO BE EVERY DAY.

Cast aside your feelings of powerlessness and understand that you run on the programming that you allow in. If you control most of it, it stands to

You can always pick up your needle and move to another groove.

Timothy Leery

reason that with diligent effort, you can change your input. If you change your input, your beliefs will change. Once your beliefs change, your output will naturally change.

Let's break it down.

As our first priority, we must restrict the negative input.

What do you *read*? Negative press sells newspapers, which makes them a haven for negativity.

Violence sells books, which fills most fictional bestsellers with greed, betrayal and death, emotional states on the low end of the spectrum.

Cheap sex, glamour and gossip fill the covers of most magazines. None of these topics bring you closer to your dreams.

If you fill your mind with negativity, violence and gossip, these will impact your beliefs.

Bottom-line: Junk belongs in the junkyard, not in your mind. **STOP STOCKPILING MENTAL GARBAGE.**

Constantly ask yourself this question:

"What am I letting in?"

We believe, first and foremost, what makes us feel that we are fine fellows.

Bertrand Russell

What do you *listen* to? Trash talk ratings have soared, along with the mountains of trash in our minds. Right wing commentators express biased views with no regard for tolerance or diversity.

Do you escape into the lyrics of violent songs? Do you leave the TV on in the other room? Are you buried in your own negative self-talk?

If you listen to garbage, garbage will impact your beliefs.

Ask yourself:

What are you letting in?

How many television programs hold your attention hostage? Do you *watch* inflammatory talk shows? Reality TV? Games shows? Are you a movie junkie?

Where do you think your personal life will end up if you base your ideas about relationships on soap operas or dating shows that suggest that you can find a lasting mate by process of competitive elimination?

If you watch junk, junk will impact your beliefs.

Again, ask yourself:

What are you letting in?

The world is your mirror and your mind is a magnet. What you perceive in this world is largely a reflection of your own attitudes and beliefs. Life will give you what you attract with your thoughts. Think, act and talk negatively and your world will be negative. Think, act and talk with enthusiasm and you will attract positive results.

Michael Lebeuf

Outside of familial and work related commitments, *who* captures YOUR time?

Do you surround yourself with people who bash your dreams? Do you hang out in the company of naysayers? Do you swallow and digest the advice of buddies in no better space than your own? Do your friends invite you to jump into the ditch rather than hold out a hand to help you out of yours?

Who you associate with matters—a lot. Most of us find ourselves in the identical financial bracket as our ten closest friends. We share similar relationship issues. We approach challenges (or run from them) in parallel fashion. *WE CAN'T LEARN MUCH FROM THOSE WHO KNOW NO DIFFERENT.*

It makes no sense to discuss how to make money with your perpetually broke uncle. His programming knows only one result: broke. This axiom extends to all matters.

Who you hang out with will impact your beliefs.

What are you letting in?

71

Sometimes I've believed as many as six impossible things before breakfast.

Lewis Carroll

Even your *environment* can leave a deep imprint on your programming. Depressed surroundings lead to depression. Do you drown your sorrows at the local bar? Do you hide in the stale inside of your living room? Do you lie in bed on weekends, to recover from a week of woes? Your pillow won't help you shift your programming.

Guard the gateway to your mind as if your life depended on it—because it does.

Burn the question into your consciousness.

What am I letting in?

Chapter Six

In with the new...

What you hear repeatedly you will eventually believe.

Mike Murdoch

To complete the overhaul of our belief system, we must replace the old negative input with new positive input that we personally select. This process involves conscious choice, an ongoing decision to choose input that builds you and enriches you. Over time, better input will build beliefs that support the results you want.

Let's run through the possibilities again.

Start with what you *read*.

What if you were to search out autobiographies of great women and men, study their struggles and their victories?

What if you chose personal growth authors with works full of messages of inspiration, hope and encouragement?

When was the last time you thumbed through an anthology of poetry and recited your favorite verse out loud?

Instead of joke-of-the-day, what if you subscribed to inspirational-message-of-the-day on the Internet?

The universal impulse to believe...is the principal fact in the history of the globe.

Ralph Waldo Emerson

Invest 30 minutes of your day to educate your mind. Pick a time that works best for you such as first thing in the morning or right before bed, and stick to it. Imagine that your mental library full of tabloid and sensationalist newspapers morphs into a beautiful study, with a wealth of knowledge that offers you guidance.

What you read impacts your beliefs.

Challenge yourself to ask the second key question:

"What are you putting in?"

Consider what you *listen* to.

Are you a news, sports or talk show junkie?

Do you always play the same music?

When was the last time you listened to Rachmaninoff on piano, Miles Davis on trumpet or Pavarotti singing an opera? (If you've never heard of these artists, that might be a clue.)

What if you decided to devote all of your drive time and all of your exercise time to YOU, to a new type of mental input? Listen to poetry on tape, the music of great masters, uplifting messages of renowned motivators, coaching of modern day philosophers. Little by little you will counteract

Believe one who has proved it.
Believe an expert.

Virgil

your negative programming. If you feed yourself with greatness, it will nourish your mind and soul.

Catch the news once, then plug in a great audio tape. You won't miss much during the time you give yourself to grow. The world's challenges will still thrive at the end of your daily dose of wisdom or beauty—and you'll feel better equipped to handle them.

Make a different choice. Train yourself.

What you listen to impacts your beliefs.

What are you putting in?

Consider what you *watch*. With our modern multi-media bonanza, the alternatives overwhelm us. Movies, television, cable, pay-per-view, DVDs, videos, internet broadband, the list drones on.

A VAST ARRAY OF OPTIONS DOES NOT MAKE ANY OF THEM VALUABLE.

300 channels will never guarantee that surfing will lead you to anything of merit. You must decide to make a change and go get the material yourself.

What if instead of escaping into fantasy you chose to learn from stimulating lecturers,

Penetrating so many secrets we cease to believe in the unknowable. But there it sits nevertheless, calmly licking its chops.

H. L. Mencken

documentaries that depict the wonder of nature, taped workshops designed to educate you and improve your skill sets?

What if you carefully screened the movies you took in, seeking out those with inspiring tales of overcoming odds, triumphing over oneself or learning profound lessons?

What possibilities might that plant in your programming?

Your mental computer will only absorb the data it receives. You pick that data.

What you watch impacts your beliefs.

What are you putting in?

Consider **who** shares time with you. How do they impact your programming?

Does your *"scene"* foster your dreams?

Does your family stand behind you?

Do they teach you through their example or experience?

Do you have the right coaches or tutors?

Do you have any at all?

Can you remember one amazing teacher from your youth? Most of us have had at least one,

The belief that becomes truth for me...is that which allows me the best use of my strength, the best means of putting my virtues into action.

Andre Gide

someone with a special gift that touched us in a special way. Most of us recall that person with fondness, a memory that brings a smile.

Why not re-create that successful action? Find another gifted teacher. In my opinion, the most powerful influence you will ever have to help you reach your dreams will come from embracing a mentor, or more than one. Mentors objectively bring their knowledge and wisdom to your circumstances. They offer their own experience of success as a guidebook or manual. If you communicate with them directly, they will counsel you, suggest alternatives, propose new perspectives. If you can't find one in person, select someone available to you through books, tapes and seminars. Soak up what they have to offer.

Who you follow speaks volumes about you. Success leaves clues. Greatness rubs off.

Choose your associations wisely.

They shape your beliefs.

What are you putting in?

Where do you spend your time?

Does that environment encourage you to excel?

Does it shut you down?

There are two ways to slide easily through life; to believe everything or to doubt everything; both ways save us from thinking.

Alfred Karzybski

You don't have to stay there. How many times have you felt your mood change by simply going outside, escaping from your cocoon, catching a few rays of sunshine across your brow? A dialogue in a coffee shop might lead you to a distinct point of view. A change of scenery can turn your mental grass greener.

Head to the library for a short story reading instead of happy hour with disgruntled wage earners.

Get up on Sunday morning and nourish your spirit.

Take a late night walk and spot a shooting star.

Go ice-skating, bike riding, swimming.

To be different you must first do different.

You control the physical location of **YOU**.

Remember, your mind gobbles it all.

What you do impacts your beliefs.

What are you putting in?

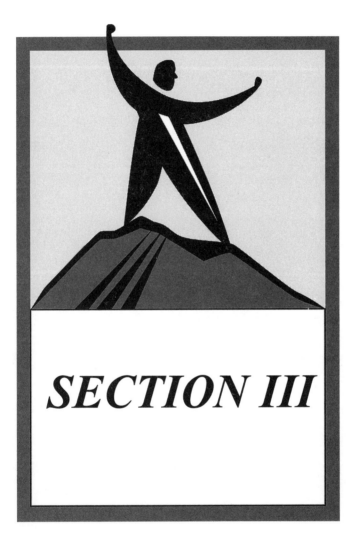

SECTION III

What if you could start over? The Release...

Imagine that you have completely changed your mental diet. You have eliminated excess fats, cut down on your sugar intake, stopped eating late at night. You drink only one cup of coffee, without cream or sugar.

Not only that, you've started to supplement with mental snacks, two or three times per day— motivational and inspirational messages, in your car and on your computer.

Your mental health improves by the minute. Your belief system is getting the kind of nutrition that it really needs. You feel hope for the first time in a long while.

Nonetheless, you carry the albatross of pre-existing beliefs, excess weight that drags you down.

That old junk has got to go.

Chapter Seven

If results don't show,

it's got to go...

They can because they believe they can.

Unknown

Assume for a moment that we implement the guidance offered by the previous two chapters. We vigilantly guard our mind's gate and carefully restrict the inflow of negativity into our belief system. We embrace positive messages of hope, beauty and inspiration and seek them out on a daily basis. What have we accomplished?

We have embarked on a massive reconstruction of our overall programming, one that can only benefit us on every imaginable level. We begin to open our eyes to new possibilities, see our options differently. We start to take small chances, commence to dream again. In a general sense, our life moves in a wonderful direction.

Congratulations. You win, as do all those you care about and all those you meet. You have taken an enormous step forward.

Empowered with knowledge and emboldened with courage, we need to kick the process up one final level. In Section One we discussed the forging of our beliefs, the building of those all-powerful wire cables reinforced by thousands of wire strands. Those cables have not snapped. They

*I make it a rule only to believe
what I understand.*

Benjamin Disraeli

continue to hold you up—in all senses of the expression. Some will feel the influence of your general re-programming set forth in Section Two. Others will remain unscathed.

If something in our lives isn't working for us, we know there must be a faulty belief in place. To manifest our truest potential and make our wildest dreams come true, we need to move from the general to the specific. Which beliefs serve me and which don't?

Imagine your life as a rich, full garden. Through general re-programming we stop the inflow of additional weeds and we sow rare and exotic plants—the seeds of big dreams.

We have one small problem. Unless we get rid of old weeds, regardless of how deep their roots have burrowed, those weeds will infiltrate and suffocate the tender buds in our garden. Our fabulous additions won't have a chance to take hold. Fragile roots will choke. The weeds will once again overrun the whole plot.

Those weeds are your mistaken beliefs.

Believe in something larger than yourself.

Barbara Bush

We need to spot them, mark them and extract them without mercy. They have no place on the portrait of your dreams.

Wait. How do we diagnose a belief as mistaken?

If we believe our beliefs, how can we pinpoint those that don't serve?

How do we gain any perspective?

We don't look at the belief itself. We scrutinize the results it produces. We judge a tree by the fruit it bears, not the fruit it ought to bear, intends to bear, hopes to bear or might bear if properly fertilized. We focus on the actual fruit and only the actual fruit.

When it comes to a belief:

If results don't show, it's got to go.

Beliefs dictate actions. Actions produce results. For the results to be right, the actions must first be right. We judge the strength (or weakness) of a belief based on its results, nothing more, nothing less.

We don't make stuff up.

We don't sugarcoat.

We don't kid ourselves.

If results don't show, it's got to go.

A belief is not true because it is useful.

Henri Frederic Amiel

Evaluating the results in your life will require courage. Certain ugly truths may seem too daunting. That's okay. As the chief architect of your palace, you have the right to change the plans, alter the foundation and modify every aspect of the entire structure. Yes, it may take time and it will most certainly take enormous effort.

Remember this:

Every faulty belief you unearth and pull out leaves you stronger and better able to manifest your full garden.

Scrutinize your results.

You don't need the weeds.

Chapter Eight

Flag it, tag it, bag it...

If you don't program yourself,
life will program you.

Les Brown

Since no one has invented magic wire cutters capable of slicing through those massive belief cables, we have no alternative but to take them apart in the same way that we put them together—one strand at a time. We will need to repeat the process over and over, and over and over, and over and over—until each non-serving belief lies on the ground in a growing pile of useless wire.

The formula for discarding mistaken beliefs involves three steps.

Step one: We must recognize when a belief doesn't serve us. We have to *FLAG IT*.

Most often, we know ourselves well enough to identify when our actions don't produce the desired results. Occasionally, we miss the boat. We must resolve to question behavior based only on its results, never on intentions or good will. We must train ourselves to maintain a constant state of vigilance, to watch our actions, stay awake and alert.

"Is what I'm doing serving me?
Am I getting what I want?"

It's okay to be selfish when asking these questions. Take no prisoners. Be adamant in your mind. Ask the questions brutally and remember—only YOU hear the answer. Why kid yourself?

Be not afraid of life. Believe that life is worth living and your belief will help create the fact.

William James

Tell the truth—yes or no.

Once you recognize an action that fails to produce the result you want, *flag it*.

Don't second guess the plan. Trust your intuition. If you get even an inkling that the results of an action fell short, *flag it*. Don't wait.

Step two: We have to identify the belief that lies behind the action we took. We have to *TAG IT*.

Once you recognize that an action fails to produce desired results, you must figure out which belief caused you to take that action in the first place. Ask yourself tough questions:

"What drove me to do that?

Why did I act that way?"

Again, no one hears the answer except you. Don't lie. Examine yourself. Take a hard look at what motivates you.

Why do you behave that way?

Where does it come from? Unearth the source. Dig it up.

"My actions stem from my beliefs. My beliefs come from somewhere. Where? What are they? What do I really feel about this? Am I fooling myself?"

My great religion is a belief in the blood, the flesh, as being wiser than the intellect. We can go wrong in our minds. But what our blood feels and believes and says is always true. The intellect is only a bit and a bridle.

D. H. Lawrence

Keep asking. Keep digging. This is your life and your future. If you don't identify your beliefs, you will never gain the power to change them.

Dig deeper.

"Who told me that? What exactly did they tell me? Did it work for them? If it did, do I have the qualities and capabilities in place so that it might work for me?"

Ask yourself again and again.

"What drives me? What drives me when it comes to relationships? What drives me when it comes to wealth and money? What drives me when it comes to health? What are my beliefs?"

Identify them, one by one. Each time you uncover a new one that doesn't **PRODUCE THE RESULTS YOU WANT, FLAG IT.**

Step three: Unravel that belief strand and *BAG IT*.

This represents both the easiest and hardest of the three steps. It's easy because as soon as you flag and tag a belief, you can easily go through the mental exercise of telling yourself:

"Nope. This one doesn't serve me. Into the bag it goes."

109

We have only to believe. And the more threatening and irreducible reality appears, the more firmly and desperately must we believe. Then, little by little, we shall see the universal horror unbend, and then smile upon us, and then take us in its more human arms.

Piere Teilhard de Chardin

It's hard because you have woven so many strands into every one of your cables that only persistent, determined effort will unwind any major belief for good. The difficulty compounds because although the winding happened in an orderly fashion, the unwinding will seem messy, haphazard, tedious and slow. The shape, form and state of the cable shifts and molds as you grow older. You must develop the skill set to unwind a belief, much more challenging than the process of winding, a more natural process.

At times the repetition may feel hopeless:

"Will this ever change?"

The answer to that question depends entirely on you. Unraveling takes amazing patience.

What if it took you ten years to convert your belief system into something that made you wealthy, prosperous and able to contribute to your community in ways other than by your own sweat and toil?

Would it be worth it?

What if it took ten years to overcome enough of your personal issues to enjoy a fabulous life-long relationship that gets better and better?

Would it be worth it?

111

A belief is not just an idea a person possesses; it is an idea that possesses a person.

Unknown

Will you enjoy many mini-victories and suffer many mini-defeats along the journey?

You bet.

So what? Consider what will happen if you don't go through the process. In fact, you already know.

Nothing. Nothing will happen.

You will find yourself parked in the exact same chair you sit in right now—except older, a little more jaded, a little more rigid in your thinking and your beliefs—a kind of arthritis of the mind.

If you do nothing to change your beliefs, nothing else will change. The faces that surround you may vary, the problems won't. You may shift your location but you won't alter your circumstances.

Take those beliefs that don't serve you and fill bag after bag. Each time one shows up, *FLAG IT, TAG IT AND BAG IT*.

Take those bags and dump them. Over time, you will bag certain beliefs before they take hold of you. You will recognize and identify them the moment they hit your consciousness. You will unravel them far more quickly. The cable will

We are inclined to believe those we do not know, because they have never deceived us.

Samuel Johnson

weaken until it finally loses its grip.

Now you gain the power.

Now you write the code.

Because you program the machine, you determine the output.

Re-write your script.

Determine a new ending.

You're in charge.

Chapter Nine

Time is on your side...

*Conduct is the ultimate test of
the worth of a belief.*

Theodore Roosevelt

In all human endeavors, greatness extracts a uniform toll. We call it time.

Rome was not built in a day and neither will a new belief system.

It took generations to build a wall around China. Generations built the wall that protects your belief system, in all its flaws and glory.

Pioneers catch most of the arrows in their back. If you lead the pack in your family, you may meet stiff opposition from those *"entrenched in their ways."*

Go about your business deliberately. Observe. We learn more by noticing behavior we dislike than by casually noting others' strong points. Disdain and scorn catch our attention. Let your loved ones become your teachers. Forgive them. Appreciate them. Don't condemn them for sheltering their beliefs. You come from the same stock, molded from the same data.

Only your conscious decision to re-program yourself will make you any different. Only you can make that decision.

119

All things are possible to him who believes.

Jesus

As you extricate yourself from those thick cables, on occasion a snag will catch you and pull on you. You may find yourself conflicted between an old belief that produced marginal results and the prospect of adopting a new one with no guaranteed outcome. Take a chance. Risk it. Put on a fresh possibility like you might wear a new coat. See how it fits. Experience how it feels. Walk around with it.

Then judge the results.

Suppose that somewhere in your history you acquired the belief that *"conflict is bad."* On the positive side, people see you as a *"really nice person."* On the negative side, you get taken advantage of fairly frequently at work.

Being overly nice gives you good results in your personal life, poor results on the job. What if you chose to keep the *"niceness"* outside the office, but don a coat of courage and stand up to the bullies at work. At first this new coat will feel funny and even uncomfortable. That's okay. Don't focus on the coat. Focus on the results that you get when you wear it.

If you like the results, keep the coat. If not, try on a different one.

You can only win. Time is on your side.

A man must not swallow more beliefs than he can digest.

Brooks Adams

Every day of self-observation, every unraveled strand, every new line of code brings you closer to self-mastery.

Make a long-term commitment. A journey of a thousand miles begins with a single step. The light shines at the end of the tunnel. Your light.

No one can express your potential except you. No outside source holds any real sway. No one defines you. No one bars you from greatness. Your programming will always produce in accordance with its code—no more, no less.

You truly are in charge, as soon as you reform your beliefs.

The data processors await your instructions. The gnomes would rather be organized and disciplined than running into each other in complete disarray. Marshall your resources, take command. The world has a funny way of making space for people who know where they are going.

You have a unique contribution to make. The world wants you to make it. The world supports abundance.

Stake a claim and start mining.

Some things have to be believed to be seen.

Ralph Hodgson

Nothing worthwhile grows overnight. Free rides feel empty when they fizzle out. Take your time, whatever time you need.

Character flows from following through on a decision long after the excitement of the moment has passed. You can do it. The furthest you have ever gone is only the beginning of how far you are capable of going.

Victor Hugo once said:

"There is one thing stronger than all the armies in the world, and that is an idea whose time has come."

Reform your beliefs.

Start now.

125

EPILOGUE

How sweet it is...

Imagine this...

You wake up in the morning, refreshed from a night of vivid dreams. With a clear and quiet mind, you greet the day.

Before you rise, you spend a few intimate moments with yourself, or with your mate, no walls, no stories, no chatter in your head.

Your beliefs serve you.

The face that gazes back at you in the mirror has a soft and relaxed quality, a confidence that doesn't foster harsh lines. You find yourself humming.

The food you feed your body pulses with life. You deserve the best, demand it and get it.

You take time for meditation or prayer, prepare yourself to create value through your daily activities.

In your studio, your work awaits you, projects bursting with creativity that require your special touch. You find innovative ways to touch the lives of your children, leave an imprint on the world that will last far beyond your days.

Your beliefs give you choices.

You plan your world.

129

No one tells you what to do. You choose.

You script your role. You play the lead.

You control the outcome, master of your mind, in charge of all programming.

You build your palace.

As the sun sets, you reflect on your day. You notice that as has become customary, you wear a smile instead of a frown.

You extend gratitude for the service you offered, the contribution you made. You carry the silent acknowledgment that you gave the world your best on this day, tipped the scales toward joy and hope.

You conjure up yet another way of sharing, wrestle with the logistics and the magnitude. "How much can I do? How much more can I give?"

You watch the fading sun dip below the horizon, turn to join your family and carry the last few rays with you. As you do each night, you celebrate the reunion.

As you tip your glass and drink in life's victories, you remember the old you and feel your inner smile broaden.

*Now, **you believe**.*

The tiny fly can indeed travel a thousand miles.

Acknowledgements

No project of any significance ever takes shape without the effort of a dynamic team and the emotional strength of a tremendous supporting cast. I have been blessed with both and though many others deserve my deepest gratitude and appreciation, I acknowledge these special people who continue, day in and day out, to inspire me:

To Annie, Ashley, Chris, David, David, Jayesh, Mark & Steve—the best Board of Advisors any country boy could ever have...

To Vito and Tara, and all of TFN, for the constant encouragement and friendship...

To Ken Atchity, my trusted counsel and coach for the last fifteen years...

To Angel and Blenda Hines, for keeping me on the straight and narrow...

To my SGI comrades, an endless source of spiritual guidance...

To Kerry Daigle, for the words of wisdom and sage advice...

To Don Fergusson, emailer extraordinaire, who always goes the extra mile...

To Tutu, Colleen and the clan who make my home a delight...

To all writers, poets, artists and dreamers who fill the universe with song—I draw from you daily and salute you with all my heart.

133

Ridgely Goldsborough